ANGLES OF APPROACH

DATE DUE

JUL 1 4 2011

ANGLES OF APPROACH

— POEMS —

Holly Iglesias

Marie Alexander Poetry Series, Volume 14

WHITE PINE PRESS / BUFFALO, NEW YORK

ACKNOWLEDGMENTS begin on page 77.

The publication of this book has been made possible by support from Robert Alexander and with public funds from the New York State Council on the Arts, a State Agency.

First Edition

Library of Congress Control Number: 2010925984

ISBN: 978-1-935210-17-7

Marie Alexander Poetry Series, Volume 14
Series Editor: Robert Alexander
Editor: Nickole Brown

Printed and bound in the United States of America.

White Pine Press
P.O. Box 236
Buffalo, NY 14201
www.whitepine.org

for Catherine

CONTENTS

Rhetoric / 11

I. NOSTALGIA

II. MENACE

III. CONFESSION

RHETORIC

You avoid breezy questions, the musings they call forth that do not pass for answers but nod, rather, toward some small intimation of a reason to be here, the black tulip plucked from a neighbor's yard, or jottings on notepaper the color of dusk when you nursed a carafe of *vin ordinaire* until the light completely faded and it was no longer safe to walk back to the hotel. You shun the phrase *body of work*, buckling at the image of your words in a satin-lined box, the family gazing at sentences, paragraphs, grief-struck but composed as they recall your writing implements, their evolutionary path from crayon to pencil, typewriter to laptop, a series akin to the March of Progress in school books that always started with an ape at the left margin, walking toward the low-browed Homo sapiens, then an erect Neanderthal, his posture promising years of hunting and gathering, the mastery of tools that will spawn pyramids, aqueducts, monasteries sacked by barbarians, Scripture translated into vulgar tongues, kings with their own churches, conquistadors claiming entire hemispheres in the middle of the page, then bolts of textiles, kegs of rum, leg irons and cotton gins, belching smoke-stacks and fireproof safes loosed upon the world by titans of industry, and finally, the barrel-chested man in a homburg checking his pocket-watch as a locomotive called The 20th Century edges toward him from the right.

I.

NOSTALGIA

CHICKEN HILL, 1943

Happy days came and went, as did the songs that Roy Price and his wife sang as they walked to the mill and back. Until the crash, until the strike that left five men dead beside the fence, until she expired birthing the girl. Two babies on his hands and nothing but a quilt to keep him company till Lillie came along, right out of the blue. How she soothed him, that woman, cooing at him, pulling lint from his hair, bearing him three more sons, all swiftly baptized by pressing their heels into a bowl of dough. Biscuits with beans, biscuits with corn: Heaven was made of this, Roy knew it, and his five children in bleached flour-sack shirts knew it too.

RUDY AND THE SCIENCE OF APPETITE

There is nothing we cannot learn, dear, nothing we cannot do, for the world is our plaything, an oyster, a horse painted blue. A sea of wheat behind us now, drays along the market road, boys in a hired buggy behind the Grange. The swing still hanging in the orchard, where once my hands caught then pushed, caught then pushed the small of your back till your shoes reached the sky and cottonwoods sighed for love of you.

DEPRESSION GLASS

Soft as talc on the palms of the blind, your fingers tap a banister, a chair back, anything to guide you down the narrow hall of November. You were dreaming: chipped Hummels on the mantel, your fevered cheek against the mirror, and on the sill, gloating, a glue pot poised to mend what's best left asunder: shards of Dresden, tattered hearts, that crock of grief pickling in the cellar.

KINETICS AND THE TRAINING OF THE EYE

The biograph is plagued with vibration; the pictures refuse to rest. A million images swarm the screen, the swell of desire like a river in spring, objects swept into the current—pigs, piano, steeple, rake—stoking its hunger for more and more.

FORLORN

1.

Nary a word. Hush the blanket of abandon. Eight shoes lined up at the door, tongues grooved by years of lacing. One child, two: the woman could not have borne a third, history a luxury beyond her means.

2.

Place five chickens in the yard, a colander of peas on her lap. Slam the screen door to jolt the hollyhocks from their dozing. Perhaps this is the day a block of ice will fall from the milk truck, or Mother eavesdrop on the party line.

3.

See the alley, the besotted peonies by a wooden gate. Father on his morning walk at the very point where he turns back, a point that never changes. The idea of banishment hovers like sweat bees, harmless, but still, that buzz.

MR. MERRICK'S MOTHER'S ROSE

Modest, it keeps to our side of the fence, the fence as much a joke as George's tiny wife swatting mosquitos with a tea towel. Futile, really, such niceties in a malarial swamp. First it was grapefruits, then coontie starch, and now it's land, pure and simple, little plots for the common man, the New Man with his celluloid collar and factory wage hoping to buy a piece of the City Beautiful on margin. A minister's son has no business doing business, but mine is to mind my tongue, tend the flowers and clip the roots dangling from strangler figs before they take over the lawn.

CONCEPTUAL ART

An act of recovery, they call it, curators rooting through the baggage of inmates deposited long ago for safekeeping, hungry for narratives free of consequence. In a small strapped case, the single starched shirt, his winter drawers, a geography text once memorized to win the ribbon Mother tacked to the parlor wall, boasting of her genius boy. Before he began drooling in church, tweezing the hairs from his forearm, singing to himself as he walked to the foundry after a breakfast of oats and beans and splashing his cheeks with her cologne. Before he started seeing things that weren't there and begged her for stories in Polish to soothe his fears, his grief for uncles buried in an old world and the name no one in town could pronounce. He lived out the balance of his days in gray pants and black shoes, took meals at six, twelve, and six, and dug graves when told to. His single pleasure, if you dare call it that, the school book: a quiet, solid thing upon his lap each afternoon, his fingers, smooth as the pages, patting it, stroking it, calming the tempest between its covers.

PROJECTOR

Motor whirring, screen emitting a smell like floor wax, Brother's fist in front of the lens, blotting out Aunt Ruth's head as she extends the pickle dish for the camera to see. Dust in the tube of light, antic as 8 mm film.

Children in the dark, untouched by war and all the parents know but never say. They stare at the rush of images—birthday cakes, Mother's prize roses, a red Schwinn—jittery icons to comfort them in some future Babylon.

NOSTALGIA FOR THE GREEN OF THE RIVER, THE WHITES OF HIS EYES

You rinse with bleach, smell like smoke, eat beans from a can. You pray for sleep and measure time by clouds that skim the pond. You drink with strangers, recite the names of trees and weeds to forget the scorching stoops of summer. You crawl in cellar holes, weep for mint and rambling rose, for tattered curtains and tilting barns and depleted stock, your history elsewhere, a distant orchard tangled with suckers. You step over plot lines, abandoning what was yours, and see how you came, when he died, into nothing.

SERMONETTE

This morning I take as my text the third book of Ralph, where we learn of his wanderings and the conversation with demons on the open road that led to his first conversion—yes, his first, for there were to be many more, and yes again, because for him conversation was The Way, not the books by which we remember him, those most silent of conversations, but the garrulous meander that flowed so easily in the presence of strangers, that river of words with no apparent source which was—amen—the route to redemption as surely as Paul's fall from his horse or Thomas's probe of the Most Precious Wound.

SPIN CYCLE

Pin curls under a dime store scarf, orange blossoms and mermaids on a field of blue. She goes to the basement of a house that was pasture two years ago, laundry now an indoor affair. No willow basket, no sheets on the line, just diapers sloshing behind a tiny porthole.

She lights a cigarette, considers throwing herself upon the machine, white enamel cool against her skin in a dance of agitation. Instead she fills a Pepsi bottle with water, taps a finger to the iron. Today is Tuesday: shirts, heavy starch.

THE DEAD OF WINTER

Hair shorn, I join the penitents, the long line of collaborators stretching from one end of the century to the next. In the windowpane, my parents battle for my face: his chin, her eyes, his exhaustion, her wit. Once, I was their playground, their double feature, the audience as they danced in the kitchen to Tommy Dorsey, Scotch and Pablum side by side on the counter. We were the lucky ones; every sign bore it out—the patio slabs, the TV dinners and iron lungs, the heaps of magazines with snapshots of bathing beauties and swiftly executed spies. But they spent their hearts like spare change, and death, when it came, found them in separate beds.

PERISHABLES

In the final days of the war, a boy eats cake, a cake from the saddest mother, a woman unaware that her own son has bled into history, a history with jaws that are soft and tropical, the greenest green, not gray like Lake Erie in winter.

The cake sealed first in waxed paper, then gift wrap, then a grocery bag dismantled with pinking shears, the bundle tied with cotton string, her fingers recalling the tiny buttons of his school shirts, the comb dipped in water before parting his hair.

Mercy rains at every latitude, at each contested parallel, rains anywhere that grunts line up for salt pills, clean socks, for unclaimed parcels that go to those who never get mail.

Cake sweetens the mouth of a boy the woman will never meet, a boy who tastes in the kindness of strangers the complications of survival, a boy who in manhood will crumble each time he tells the tale.

PARLOR

This American life contains no meadow, no pony, no point of view, just bureaus stripped of all but the basics—safety pins, smelling salts, violet pastilles, all the random what-nots skittering in the recesses of a drawer with each push and pull. Perhaps what is called for is a yard of linen, the heavy satin stitch of a monogram, something soft, like a damper.

KINDLING

When the end came, the surprise was that it was no surprise. No shrieks, no stampede, just calm: the sky red and droning, banks of smoke, silver flecks floating in the air like snow. Report of it came like a bundle daring to be opened, within it all that was shattered then gathered, a curse.

Survivors crawled out of cellars to watch it, to face the end they knew had come, a world unmoored from past and future, which should not surprise you, you who were birthed in the beauty of ruin.

II.

MENACE

MIDDLE OF NOWHERE

The idea of Kansas fills the screen—November, windbreak of trees—a foil to the city without which there is no heartland, no horror. We scan the fields until the camera sets a building in its sights, walks us toward it to show the clean lines, the white solidity of a farmhouse through blades of wheat. We hear an impossible rustle, want to muffle it, for silence is essential to notions of prairie. Were there a scarecrow or stalks of corn, we could not be more certain that we had arrived at the great middle, the plain, awful core of it all. Or that we are about to happen upon stains, small pools of extinguished life darkening the floorboards.

LITTLE ICE AGE; OR, THE NEW RELIGION

1.

Shoeless saints, celibate saints, saints soft as bonbons dot the landscape, the millennial highway choked with monks in robes that rasp their thighs, Everyman itching for indulgence as the plagues of pus and profit plow through.

2.

Destiny's manifest on a tradewind. Lobal warning. Questions of safe passage and papal bull. And what of the barbarian's stammer, surest sign of damnation?

3.

Flesh and magic banished, modesty and capital take flight. Instruments of precision yielding not one map, but two.

4.

Goodwife fingers an empty purse; a boy sticks his head in a pot. The apprentice fans a brazier heaped with dead coals. Amidst the clutter of his trade, the alchemist wonders: What is lost in the refinement of metal, and what in the pursuit of gain? Chance dances on Virtue's grave. The almshouse awaits them all.

DULLE GRIET / MAD MEG

Egg flecks in the dishwater. China stacked at table's edge. A ham sweating on the counter as the woman dreams of having her say and eating it too.

She puts an onion in the blender, and with it a cup handle, two teaspoons and her wedding ring.

Finger to the switch—her finest hour—she pushes the buttons. Chop, grind, purée.

FROM *THE LIVES OF THE SAINTS*:
THE MEEK IN DEATH SHALL BLEED

Germaine, an unsightly child with withered hands and scrofulous neck, had but French and faith, the Angelus and self-mortification as her daily joys. A girl, in short, of the times. Streams parted before her, roses spilled from her lap, and God was so pleased with the miserable creature that He called her to heaven before she could kiss the sixteenth century goodbye. The night sky pierced by His radiance as virgins led the villagers to the barn where the body lay. Magnificent in death as in deprivation, she defied decay through the ages, till the Reign of Terror and quicklime finally did the trick.

HOLY SEE

Eggs sputter in the pan like static. In the highchair a boy too big for it, a boy who will never walk but dreams of soccer shoes just the same. Spatula drawn, his mother waits for the quivering to cease, the surrender of clarity as the yellow eye sets.

In the shadow of giant transmitters, Santa Maria di Galeria is a swarm of sound: Mass in ten languages, lamps flickering like martyrs on a spit, and on the hour the Pope's voice emanating from ovens up and down the streets.

LITTLE WOMEN

The utopian sentence a forced march, sisters with baskets of darning slung on their hips, Mama minding the sick, evening but a stitch in the hem of war. Uncivil, disobedient, they slip like hankies into pockets of tomfoolery. The Sage of Concord, deaf to the chatter of girls, different drummers thundering in the plush case of his brain, takes up his pen. Today: circles.

SAINT OF SHENANIGANS

On the lip of dark ages, a canker, a queen of deceit, her felicitous tongue but babble to boys fattened on empire. Fidgety quick, she feeds a hem inch by inch to the ravenous needle, hair littered with pins and lint, shirtwaist crusted with starch for modesty's sake. *The sass of that girl, a mouth that won't quit. Barbarians, the lot of them, filthy Harps, always drunk or saying their beads.*

Oh Bridget, we pray ye, spare us the Know-nothings, their nativist spleen. Grant us patience to soothe the rage-racked heart.

THE PANIC OF NINETY-THREE

Stockings rinsed, shirts ironed, sheets hung by the Seckel pear that is the woman's delight. Baby, a girl, the fifth in as many years, lolling beside the willow basket, loop-headed as a lamb. Patches of grass sprouting in the mud, goats banging against the pen.

The child rises, takes her first steps across the flat field of Illinois. Mama turns in surprise, her skirts stirring a breeze: Papa, home from the bank before noon.

GILDED

Bloody roast, Madeira toasts, Cuba and Guam like watch fobs on a golden chain. Tonics for neurasthenics, manifestos and gruel for the rest.

> *We don't want to fight,*
> *But by Jingo! if we do,*
> *We've got the ships,*
> *We've got the men,*
> *And we've got the money too.*

A progressive income tax, perhaps, something to serve as a sop.

BOOM

First the world glitters with the grit of things blown from the cupboard, closet, garage. Then Mom and Pop, Brother and Sis settle in to read, to listen to the radio, to wolf down canned spaghetti and applesauce, to play shadow games till the batteries wear out.

Thus begins the dreaming, the long mushroom night.

CODDLED

Father long gone. Mother shuffling across the linoleum, flustered, scraping toast, watching the timer, the kettle.

She ties the Sweetie Pie bib around my neck and spoons the egg, loose and vague, from its shell into my bowl.

Gums clamped, my four teeth mere nubs, I will not eat it.

THE HIERARCHY OF FRUITS

We learned the virtue of apples, of firm flesh and uniform color. We diagrammed the passive voice, sang Gregorian chants, and charted personal hygiene habits as an exercise in science because there were no monkeys in space yet. We watched filmstrips and pondered limbo and the fate of pagans, those grinning, naked people who ate termites for breakfast but did not know God. Surely they got the better deal, dancing and climbing trees and eating with their hands, while we sat at metal desks, decked in plaid and guarded like grenades with faulty pins.

KITCHEN CONVERSION

Yolk coagulating on a blue plate, blackbird on the sill. On her lap a book and in the book ten tales of scolds with bored tongues, busy-bodies beside themselves with prophesy, robbing enthusiasm of its good name, toting to the New World old pots where they simmered roots and knuckles, spooned marrow into wounded mouths to test for the trace of abomination.

CIVIL DEFENSE DRILL NO. 6

Her life grew inflamed, like gums around a tooth that needs pulling, the swelling an impediment to digestion and speech. And so she made pap of her sentences, dipped the tip of Baby's spoon into it, imploring her to open big, to swallow, these small supplications but the first in a series that teach a mouth to take what's given—*Say ah!*—*ah* the portal to tongue depressor, swab, dogma, and drill.

DOMESTIC BLISS

Graciela sweeps. She irons. She rubs wax into the piano keys. She eats crackers under a banyan, then rinses her hands in the pool.

Graciela has one name only, takes wages in cash. Her husband drives a bread truck and on Saturdays they eat what's left.

Graciela says, *Mistolín berry-berry nice. Lady,* she cries, flushing the toilet twice for the joy of it, *¡Mira que limpo!*

LIMIT YOUR SEARCH

"How to stop wanting what you can't have" yields zero results. "Wanting what you can't have," hundreds, like "drugs are a crutch you must lay at His feet" and eleven stanzas on *Poetry Daily* about some guy groping a brunette in the back of a '66 Ford pickup in a corn field. My father was right: naming an entire generation after a soft drink was the first step on the road to ruin. "What you can't have" opens the flood gates—sales charts, pressure points, the Hip Slenderizer, an angry god, control issues, moral fiber, emergency evacuation, a persistent rash. "How to stop."

SEASON OF THE WITCH

The shift blows in, rattles the trees, sets leaves to whispering tenuous thoughts, shreds of dreams, as though they too had trusted lyric's impulse before epic kicked the door down, sized up the interior, and found it lacking.

Only the photos in matching frames suffice, generations shelved in proper order, dressed in clothes they can't afford, each wedding attached to a war, the wars tumbling onto each other like dominoes of romance—bride, groom, bride, groom, bride, groom, bride.

FREIGHT

Each face turns away, a hand cupped over the brow to shade eyes that no longer close. Each body standing—how could it be otherwise—no one can rest.

Silence settles in. The crowd swells, solidifies, a wall of clothes—shirts, shoes, pants in black and blue, aprons, socks, vests and smocks and sorry belts that cinch what little is left of them.

Tracks approach, rails that haul them into our field of vision. We who wait at unforeseen stations, we whose mouths avoid words fouled by history. Hygiene. Boxcar. Furnace.

SOAP

She was a housewife with a typewriter, the type of gal who stared at the lawn through the steam of a percolator, watched rush hour carry the men away with their cuff links and Chiclets and pockets full of dimes. Who composed church bulletins and occasional verse, manifestos and inflammatory prose, fingers electric as they tapped on the keys. Who left cigarettes smoking on the edge of the sink, scripting flimsy narratives in the air—Drift, Ivory, Cashmere Bouquet—as she scraped away years of wax to discover the floor's true color.

III.

CONFESSION

MASS FOR THE HAPPY DEATH OF INNOCENCE

Girls sashaying to the drugstore for smokes, for mint pastilles and Betadyne; lunch-counter ladies sucking their teeth, dabbing sweat from their lips with lavender handkerchiefs, pouring more chicory for Father Poché, poor soul, too late for communion, too early for Scotch. *Candy man has come and gone, oh my candy man has come and gone.* Boys hide in the trees, in trees that never lose leaves, boys drinking beer who jeer and flirt and whisper nasties onto the hats of passersby. A girl presses the small of her back against a tree, cocks one foot behind the ankle of the other, the very air an invitation to spoil, Carnival just a place between the legs. Air, the air that rarely moves, damp as anything in the mouth, and leaves that never fall. A single blossom of tea olive, white, the size of a pinkie nail, gives off a scent that can buckle a grown man's knees, plant the idea of sex-right-now behind his eyes. Shoes melting into the mud, the tar on the street, odors evolving with progress up or down Canal Street, Annunciation, Calliope. Standing in the shade, heels sunk in the soft soil of the neutral ground, a woman fingers a token, her friend rolling crisp white paper down the length of a baguette, offering a bite as the trolley approaches, its wheels clacking, sparks flying high and low.

Like a scar from a thousand whippings, the levee rises between river and peril, young men high on the swell of it taking their leisure. Stuck with schoolyard names—Bobby, Baby, Jimmy D—they consider themselves boys, always will, even when lifting the skirt of a wife, a mistress, a forbidden young thing. Everything that sloshes in a bottle of pink Chablis smiles on them, gives the nod to their antics as sun bronzes the water. Come dusk, they depart, gallants on the prowl for cherry-studded cocktails and girls who straddle stools like they can't get enough of anything, who booze with boys through an eternal childhood of damp air and the Tropics' imperative to couple. The only breeze enters the bar from a tiny window to the street, where pedestrians buy pints of Crown Royal and rye. Clawing the vinyl bumper, a weathered woman goes for the record, six Skip 'n' Go Nakeds, while the one who never eats, who never comes inside, stumbles into a metal cart of a vendor yelling, *Red Hots! Get 'em while they're red hot!* through clouds of steam. Eventually one day becomes the next and truth squats at the curb, blue as a bruise, as Jesuits move from *lait chaud* in the refectory to desks piled with arcana, waiting till lunch to switch to the hard stuff.

River like a slug in June, mud and more mud passing by, silt for the Delta, memory scoured from banks upriver, from territories once French and Indian, St. Louis regent of the upper valley, New Orleans the queen below. Imagine then the moment of purchase, the swift exchange of documents and flags, Toussaint and Napoleon menacing the freshly minted borders, the snits and snares of surrender to the bawdy boy of a nation set on conquest. A small army dispatched to measure mountains, to gather pelts and seed pods, to list the names of tribes on the journey west, thick-tongued mercenaries misinterpreting the nuances of fealty, front men for speculators who could reduce the filigree of Creole society to knots on a surveyor's rope. The tourist is to believe that what remains of this plot is a flair for gracious living, nostalgic tidbits of burnt sugar served on doilies in the Quarter. But each Steamboat Gothic, every shotgun and project holds a secret, some hoodoo against the invader scrawled on wallpaper, stashed beneath the floorboards, locked in a pantry. The city itself settles deeper into that great bowl where all worlds—new and old, first and third—splash about.

Point your shoes where you want to go. Only in this way will you know direction in a land that sloughs itself daily, where tiny territories slip between your toes and seasons exceed meaning, just bloom and rain, rain and bloom, no gap between Carnival and Lent, Lent and Carnival, where upriver and down are the cardinal points, till the storm comes that changes the destiny of water, the current reversed like an infant refusing birth, aching back toward the warm and murky middle.

Bend down here; stroke the print of lovers in the sodden grass, a heel here, a knee there, the weight of their ardor in the aftermath. Watch the bodies of August wash by and know your turn will come. Pray now for those on foot, that they make the bridge by sundown, that they cross over, mercy! cross over for good.

FLOP HOUSE

Picture him pushing away from the bar, from the vinyl bumper and the red-head, before he heads home, Rusty Nails calming the benzedrine in his blood as he drives toward the glare of sunset. *Ciao, baby-doll!*

Now picture the wife, mildly tanked herself, as she stirs chili—*I'll serve it in a tureen!* Card tables set with tally pads and mixed nuts, the children in pajamas whining *It's still light outside!* till she offers them Shirley Temples, chirping *Bottoms up, you little rascals!*

DESTINY MEASURED IN CUPS

Total immersion is one thing, going *under* quite another. It is true that sex changed everything, that we escaped our mothers' fate—the Crisco and Miltown, the rocket bras and Miss Americas with big hair—but we first had to drown in language before learning how to swim.

NAYSAYER'S APPRENTICE

I went to him an awkward thing, cautious of drugstore dramas, of Brut cologne and Teaberry gum, of Gentian violet and his formulary of cures for snake bite and catarrh, but nothing for festering love. Worshipping the same woman, we passed our days floating schemes in a camphor cloud, Lister trampling through beds of narcissus, the father of antisepsis proclaiming to rows of ranch houses the triumph of romance.

THE BIRTH OF RANCH DRESSING

The time for French had passed. Gone the lettuce wedge drenched in orange, gone the Lucky Penny salad. Mother had changed, switched to Hidden Valley, inside the cruet something impossibly white, something that moved her to squeal, *It's ranch! It's homemade!* and left us wondering what ranch, what state, though we suspected Nevada, troubled by the thought of her in Western togs, flirting with cowpokes as she pondered divorce from our father.

THEORY OF FLIGHT

We watched frat boys chug can after can of Dixie beer, waiting for them to puke so we could finally kiss hope goodbye, get into cars with them and drive along the levee till the gas ran out. Our parents no longer asked where we'd been, and we no longer told them our bodies were battlegrounds beyond consecration. Long before the Summer of Love, we retreated into fantasy, stitching verse into our hems, rolling joints with a holy card, dancing with strangers at honky-tonks along the river road.

ANNUNCIATION STREET

The house lists, a steamboat beached in the Garden District, laden with cargo from other worlds—sugar, pestilence, the currency of flesh. Her eyes lock onto the back of a sleeping head as she bolts for the door, past the bed, the table, the evidence upon it—trolley token, Kools, a broken cup. But this is not the set of a movie so much as its plot. She descends the stairs, angles across the chipped, white face of decay, each step a departure as dawn drains of color like a body new to sex.

MY SEXUAL REVOLUTION

Outside the K&B, corner of St. Charles and Napoleon, Patsy Kelly pauses, pops plastic bubbles in the pink birth control case between her fingers. For months I've watched her spray the blonde bouffant, adjust the push-up bra, horny and confident as she cuts through this swamp of Jesuits and jasmine where girls are expected to show shame and cleavage in equal measure.

Now the gallant, I swagger beside her, down aisles of cold cream and aspirin, Band-Aids and Milk Duds, to the prescription counter, where she slams the case on the counter as though laying down a full house. *Charge it, Pop,* she says to the druggist. *And a pint of Jack, too.*

TO SAY AGAIN

To say again *goodbye* is to grab for the rail, tripping on the cuffs of pants made for someone taller, wary of waking the dreamers.

To remember both sides of the door, the peephole glowing like an unnamed planet, the house a galaxy unto itself.

To know the curb, the gutter, the gurgle of sewers after April's inevitable flood.

FOUND: A SORROW SONG

Oh, St. Louis, such a colored town, minefield of myth and memory. The Negro must give the world his side of the awful story, the writhing of an age translated to black.

Inevitable seeds, harvest of disaster. Oh, St. Louis, the smirch upon us, murder condoned as people sit silently by. Kind missionary, come back and convert these Christians!

The past still performing itself, tragedy pushed to its bitter end. The color line, American heartbreak deep as a river. Oh, St. Louis, such a colored town, my field of myth and memory.

FROM THE FINAL BOOK OF RALPH

1.

I stood before him scowling, unwilling to twirl the petticoat, to fold down the cuffs of my pastel socks. *Stylish,* he said, my father's attempt to appease me, tease me into believing that girlhood was a piece of cake, a gas, a romp.

2.

At the drugstore, I was free to try on sunglasses, lipstick, cologne, until he yelled, *Time to go, kiddo!* and I followed him, that man with all the keys, I followed him out the door and into the night, as though we were both destined for happiness.

3.

Old Spice, nosegays, bloody roast beef, the father-daughter banquets were costume dramas of things to come, my old man the only cool cat there, the one who played Louis Prima on the hi-fi and taught me how to drink Scotch neat, the one I drove home as he sobbed into his sleeve, *Your mother's one hot ticket.*

4.

Now, every day is the day he died—not the Saturdays off, king of the garage in plaid shorts, not the single day I call childhood, when we burned trash at the curb and watched sparks fly, not the Sunday I gave birth in a language he didn't speak, not the morning he pulled the dialysis needle from his arm, the sheet suddenly sprinkled like a suburban lawn, pleading, *Please get me, please get me, God, get me out of here.*

MORIR SONAÑDO: TO DIE DREAMING

1.

Vultures circle high above the Federal Building, while below, appetites bulge like wallets, each sign a lure. SPY STORE! ¡COMPRAMOS ORO! The Americas couple in broad daylight, a dance of hemispheric attraction, the tiny waist between north and south clenched in the embrace of rough trade.

2.

Fidelity's just monkey business in a town where fishing boats double as motels and a former Miss America cites The Good Book to damn queers but not mermaids on water skis or pipe bombs in mailboxes, the moon looming low all the while, white as a cream pie in the hands of a clown.

GOODWILL OFFERING

I toss the comforter at the town dump, the remains of a childhood that ended when I sewed nametags into her clothes, when she read from the handbook. "Rules for the Phone," "Visits to Chapel," chapel the one place a girl might hide in the hush of private sorrows.

No one weeps for the young; they're too beautiful to need our tears. They bear what they're given and sleep like stones. If they remember us at all, it is as shadows, not as guardians who failed them, toting their suitcases, handing them over to strangers for safekeeping.

TURBULENCE

You toss on the sea of yourself, praying for rest as photos of forebears who refuse to claim you stare from across the room. Outside, everywhere, the profusion of late spring—pollen, peepers, peonies tumbling like drunken bridesmaids.

Sleep, now. Dream of sheets pressed in a mangle, of pillows dense enough to take the weight of your head, of windows opening onto the night of their own accord.

TRIPPING

We enter the great bowl between Stockbridge and South Dakota, where all that is east or west drains into a single river. Wandering from donut to taco, coffee to Coke, the miles accrue like indulgences as we snack our way through Ohio, past rusted plows and Old Country Buffets and acres of portaletes. Without warning, the radio speaks, Dr. Laura shaming a caller to stop whining and do what needs to be done, solid advice when taking the Midwest at eighty miles an hour, the ten-story cross on a grassy knoll— mercy, mercy me—but a blur as we pass.

CATHERINE'S WHEEL

If sainthood were sexy, then virtue would kneel. Teresa of Avila has nothing on you, dear, not the languid eyes Bernini gave her nor the bisque neck arched toward a vision of body made bread.

Kissing, we convert, turn to arduous pleasures, knowing that in moving we are removed, lifted skyward by the hair, God approaching as two mouths.

WEAR AND TEAR

Moonfall behind the ridge, light paling the trees, our arms reaching in prayer to pull heaven down. Here we sit, clothed in the work of others, of people with hands stained the color of our pants—curry, ocean, midnight, seed. History an ill fit, the season's upon us—time to take up the needle, mend the seam of another day.

EX LIBRIS

Unlike the sock who mistook static for love, love, passion is never lost. We may empty the house, stripping art from the walls, boxing cups and diction- aries, albums and coats, but the fervor of our days will remain, sparks rid- ing the air like dust before settling on the new owner's book, the story changed each time she averts her eyes.

OLD HAT

Land's sake, the great aunts said over tea, the light behind them dappled, filtered through a riot of vegetation on the sun porch, bristling ferns, philodendron that snaked along the sills, moss lacing into the litany that nudged time along.

More's the pity.

My, my.

Saints be praised.

NOTES

"Mr. Merrick's Mother's Rose"
George Merrick developed Coral Gables, one of the first planned communities in the United States, during the Florida land boom of the 1920s.

"Conceptual Art"
Inspired by the New York State Museum's exhibit, "The Lives They Left Behind: Suitcases from a State Hospital Attic," which featured belongings found in storage at the Willard Psychiatric Center, which closed in 1995.

"Middle of Nowhere"
The 2005 film, *Capote*, about Truman Capote investigating the 1959 murder of the Clutter family in Kansas, was shot primarily in Manitoba.

"*Dulle Griet* / Mad Meg"
A figure from Flemish legend, she is the subject of the 1562 painting by the same name by Pieter Brueghel the Elder.

"Holy See"
North of Rome, near the town of Santa Maria di Galeria, is a six-antenna cluster built in the 1950s to transmit Vatican Radio. Recent accusations by government officials claim that the transmitter has caused electromagnetic pollution in the area and that its powerful wattage is in violation of national radiation standards.

"Found: A Sorrow Song"
Sources for the words and phrases are John Keene, Ida B. Wells, W.E.B. Dubois, Mark Twain, and Langston Hughes.

ACKNOWLEDGMENTS

Thanks to the editors and publishers of the following journals, anthologies and chapbooks, where these poems first appeared, some in slightly different form.

Arts & Letters: The Panic of Ninety-three
Beloit Poetry Journal: Civil Defense Drill No. 6
Bloom: Conceptual Art
Connotation Press: An Online Artifact: Depression Glass, From *The Lives of the Saints:* the Meek in Death Shall Bleed, Kitchen Conversion, and Annunciation Street
Del Sol Review: Forlorn, Parlor, Limit Your Search, *Morir Soñando:* To Die Dreaming
Double Room: Holy See
Green Mountains Review: The Hierarchy of Fruits
Hamilton Stone Review: Kindling, Boom, Middle of Nowhere, Wear and Tear
Hands-on Saints (chapbook, Quale Press): From *The Lives of the Saints:* The Meek in Death Shall Bleed; Saint of Shenanigans
Margie: Perishables
MiPoesias: Domestic Bliss
New England Watershed Magazine: Little Women
nidus: Nostalgia for the Green of the River, the Whites of His Eyes
Prairie Schooner: Naysayer's Apprentice
Red Line Blues: Chicken Hill, 1943; The Dead of Winter; Season of the Witch
Sweeping Beauty: Contemporary American Women Poets Do Housework (University of Iowa Press): Spin Cycle, Flop House, The Birth of Ranch Dressing
U.S. Latino Review: Little Ice Age; or, the New Religion
Web del sol (online chapbook): My Sexual Revolution, Destiny Measured in Cups, Flop House
Wisconsin Review: To Say Again, Goodwill Offering

Most importantly, I wish to express my deep gratitude to Robert Alexander for his confidence and enthusiasm; to Catherine Reid, Gary Copeland Lilley, Sebastian Matthews, Susie Patlove and Kim Garcia for insightful readings of the manuscript that nurtured it toward completion; and to the North Carolina Arts Council for the generous support of an artist's fellowship.

ABOUT THE AUTHOR

Holly Iglesias is the author of *Souvenirs of a Shrunken World* (Kore Press), a collection of poems focused on the 1904 World's Fair, and a critical work, *Boxing Inside the Box: Women's Prose Poetry* (Quale Press). She teaches at the University of North Carolina–Asheville and has received fellowships from the North Carolina Arts Council, the Edward Albee Foundation, and the Massachusetts Cultural Council.

The Marie Alexander Poetry Series

Founded in 1996 by Robert Alexander, the Marie Alexander Poetry Series is dedicated to promoting the appreciation, enjoyment, and understanding of American prose poetry. Currently an imprint of White Pine Press, the series publishes one to two books annually. These are typically single-author collections of short prose pieces, sometimes interwoven with lineated sections, and an occasional anthology demonstrating the historical or international context within which American poetry exists. It is our mission to publish the very best contemporary prose poetry and to carry the rich tradition of this hybrid form on into the 21st century.

SERIES EDITOR: ROBERT ALEXANDER
Editor: NICKOLE BROWN

Volume 14
Angles of Approach
Holly Iglesias

Volume 13
Pretty
Kim Chinquee

Volume 12
Reaching Out to the World
Robert Bly

Volume 11
The House of Your Dream:
An International Collection of Prose Poetry
Edited by Robert Alexander and Dennis Maloney

Volume 10
Magdalena
Maureen Gibbon

Volume 2
Your Sun, Manny
Marie Harris

Volume 1
Traffic
Jack Anderson